Misty's Mini Guides

LAKELAND WALKS FOR BIG DOGS!

Series 2 - Central & East Cumbria

Sharon Leedell

Published in 2020 by Sharon Leedell

Icons courtesy of FREEPIK

ISBN: 978-1-9162758-7-4

Printed in the UK by INGRAM
Book & Cover Design by Russell Holden

Pixel Tweaks Publications
SELF PUBLISHING MADE SIMPLE

www.pixeltweakspublications.com

A Catalogue record for this book is available from the British Library.

Printed by Ingram

Front cover - Path to Easedale
© Sharon Leedell 2020

Cumbria is a mountainous area and can be dangerous with fast-changing weather. The paths may be rocky, slippy and/or steep. For your own safety we recommend the wearing of hiking boots and other suitable outdoor clothing for mountainous regions. The routes detailed in these guides are meant to be used in conjunction with an OS map & compass for the area, or a suitable GPS device. Farming practices may change over time, and sheep may be moved!

This book is dedicated, with grateful thanks,
to Alyson Revens and Peter Hyde, without
whom we would never have met our fur-baby
Misty or the lovely Laney

ACKNOWLEDGEMENTS

Thanks to mum and dad for getting me into
fell walking at an early age

To Bob Pain for being my rock and
encouraging me with all my mad ideas

And thanks to Russell Holden of Pixel Tweaks
for his great enthusiasm and for making this
book a reality!

Introduction

Welcome to the second book in our series, made specially for owners of large dogs that cannot get over stiles! The first book covered our favourite walks around North and West Cumbria, and this one concentrates on East and Central Cumbria.

The walks are all ones we have explored either jointly or by myself as an 'exploratory mission'. They are usually up to 8 miles long, (though some have optional shorter routes) and we think they deserve the paw of approval for big dogs!

As a keen amateur photographer, I've also chosen walks with the most superb views, which I hope you and your furry companions will enjoy as much as we did!

Sharon

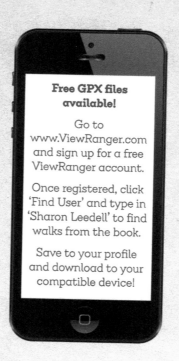

Free GPX files available!

Go to www.ViewRanger.com and sign up for a free ViewRanger account.

Once registered, click 'Find User' and type in 'Sharon Leedell' to find walks from the book.

Save to your profile and download to your compatible device!

When using GPX files, please be aware that whilst every care has been taken to ensure accuracy, the route may not exactly match the path on the ground.

COVID-19 UPDATE

During the current pandemic it's important to keep a safe distance from others and be aware that some facilities, such as toilets, car parks, etc may not be open as they were at the time of writing. Please check before you travel for the current Government guidelines, and on the National Trust and local websites for the latest local facility information. You can help to keep yourself and others safe by washing your hands thoroughly with hand sanitiser regularly during the day, and especially before and after touching gates, stiles, door handles, and car park machines, and avoiding crowded areas or places where you have to squeeze past people, such as on narrow ridges.

Blue Green Algae

You may have read a lot about this in the news. This is an algae which looks (as the name suggests), like a kind of blue-green slime on the surface of the water. It can be harmful to pets and humans, so do look out for signs posted around lakes and other waterways. You can also look on the Environment Agency Twitter feed (@EnvAgencyNW) or email: enquiries@environment-agency.gov.uk

Blue green algae
courtesy of the Environment Agency

If you notice algae in the water but there are no signs, don't let your dog enter the water, and don't enter it yourself either. Instead, please telephone the incident line on 0800 80 70 60 and report it.

Sheep

Cumbria is essentially a farming community, and the sheep are often scattered around randomly on the fells. Not always visible at first, they can suddenly appear in bracken or from behind boulders or bushes. Dogs can be tempted to chase these, especially at lambing time, even if they don't chase sheep in your own local area, so care must be taken to keep your dog under close control at all times. Farmers do have the right to kill any dog seen worrying or hurting sheep, so we strongly recommend the use of a lead to keep your furry friend safe. **Always pick up after your dog and please don't leave poo bags lying around!**

SHEEP **CATTLE** **DEER**

We have indicated places you may encounter livestock in the margins with a warning symbol.

Sheep Ticks

Sheep ticks have been known to cause Lyme disease so do check your dog and yourself over after every walk and remove any found using a proper tick removing tool. Your vet or doctor can also do this for you if you are unsure.

Safety on the Hills & the Countryside Code

Whilst walking in the fells is great fun and good for the soul, it can also be very dangerous, so if you're new to hiking, here are a few tips and a mention of the Countryside Code to help you get started!

» If you are unsure or feel unsafe at any time, always turn back. The fells will be there another day! Make sure you are too!! Wear suitable clothes and footwear which are made for mountainous regions (not jeans).

» Don't try to cross fast flowing rivers or rivers in spate after heavy rain, you may be swept away – find a safe route.

» Take maps/guidebook and a compass/GPS device and know how to use them! Don't forget spare batteries!

» Do learn to read a map and compass! You can find a free, easy to follow guide on the Ordnance Survey website at: www.ordnancesurvey.co.uk/documents/resources/map-reading.pdf

» Be prepared for sudden changes in weather. The weather higher up the fell will be colder and possibly windier than down in the valley, and the conditions can change within minutes – carry warm spare clothing and waterproofs!

» In winter there may be snow and ice on the ground, ensure you are properly equipped for such conditions

» Check the weather so you know what to expect, either by going online at www.mwis.org.uk or by reading signs posted in many of the local shop windows

» Let someone know where you are going, and how long you plan to be. Be sure they know what to do if you do not return on time.

» Take plenty of food and drink with you to enjoy along the way.

» Leave gates and property as you find them - farmers may leave gates open to move livestock, so if a gate is wedged open with a rock, for example, leave it be. If a gate is closed, close it behind you and check it has closed properly.

» Show respect and consideration for the wildlife, people and animals who live in the countryside, and for other people enjoying the landscape.

» Take your litter home with you, and don't leave dog poo bags lying on the ground or hanging in trees, even if you intend to pick them up on the way back. Animals could eat these causing them to fall ill or even die. And it looks unsightly for others walking the route too.

» Take nothing away but photographs and memories. Don't damage or move rocks, plants etc.

» Give wild animals and farm animals plenty of space as they can behave unpredictably - especially around dogs, and especially if they have lambs/calves.

» Be careful not to drop matches or smouldering cigarettes. Don't light fires or disposable barbeques.

» Keep dogs under close control (By law, you must control your dog so that it does not disturb or scare farm animals or wildlife). Farmers are entitled by law to kill any dog they see worrying or killing their animals.

» Always clean up after your dog and get rid of the mess responsibly. Consider buying a dickybag to contain your dog poo bags while you enjoy your walk. These can be purchased online at www.dickybag.com

» When walking on open country and common land, you must keep your dog on a short lead between 1 March and 31 July - and all year round near farm animals. If a farm animal chases you and your dog, it is safer to let your dog off the lead - don't risk getting hurt trying to protect them.

» Consider purchasing supplies and souvenirs from local shops to support the local economy.

» If you get injured, become completely lost or feel ill and unable to continue your walk, ring 999 and ask for Police then Mountain Rescue, give details of your location (preferably a grid reference) and what the trouble is. It is recommended to carry an emergency shelter in which you can await rescue as it will likely take several hours for them to reach you. A whistle and torch are also helpful, and a small first aid kit for minor cuts and blister treatments.

Have fun and stay safe!

The Routes

Keswick ◄

A66

B5322

A591

A5091

Pooley Bridge

Dockray

A592

Ullswater

Howtown

Thirlmere

Helvellyn

Beda Fell

High Street

Kirkstone Pass

Harter Fell

Grasmere

Rydal

Ambleside

A593

Windermere

N

1 2 3 4 5 6 7 8 9 10 11 12 13 14 15 16 17 18 19 20

Look for the paws!
Be careful to choose a walk suitable for your dog's fitness, breed, age and ability.

ONE PAW = easy, low level path.
TWO PAWS = easy, but slightly longer/harder than one paw walks, possibly with some climbing.
THREE PAWS = a moderate walk, usually around 6 miles long on low fells with some climbing.
FOUR PAWS = a lengthy or strenuous walk with steep bits, up to 9 miles long. *All walk distances are approximate.*

Contents

Walk 1   **Thirlmere** - 3 miles 2   Keswick   🐾

Walk 2   **Shivery Knott/Harrop Tarn** - 5 miles..........4   Keswick   🐾🐾🐾

Walk 3   **Pooley Bridge** - 9 miles..................................6   Penrith   🐾🐾🐾🐾

Walk 4   **Gowbarrow Park** - 4 miles.......................8   Penrith   🐾🐾

Walk 5   **Grisedale Valley** - 6 miles......................10   Penrith   🐾🐾🐾

Walk 6   **Sheffield Pike** - 6 miles...........................12   Penrith   🐾🐾🐾🐾

Walk 7   **Angle Tarn** - 7 miles...............................15   Penrith   🐾🐾🐾🐾

Walk 8   **Place Fell** - 5 miles.................................16   Penrith   🐾🐾🐾

Walk 9   **Silver Point** - 4 miles.............................18   Penrith   🐾🐾

Walk 10 **Swineside Knott** - 5 miles...................20   Penrith   🐾🐾🐾

Walk 11 **Stony Cove Pike** - 4 miles.................22   Grasmere   🐾🐾🐾🐾

Walk 12 **Rydal Water** - 3 miles..........................23   Grasmere   🐾🐾

Walk 13 **Easedale Tarn** - 7 miles......................24   Grasmere   🐾🐾🐾🐾

Walk 14 **Silver How** - 6 miles............................26   Grasmere   🐾🐾

Walk 15 **Loughrigg Fell** - 3 miles......................28   Grasmere   🐾🐾🐾

Walk 16 **Brothers Water** - 5 miles....................30   Penrith   🐾🐾🐾

Walk 17 **Lanty's Tarn** - 5 miles.........................32   Penrith   🐾🐾

Walk 18 **Hartsop above How** - 7 miles..............34   Penrith   🐾🐾🐾🐾

Walk 19 **Great Dodd** - 8 miles...........................36   Penrith   🐾🐾🐾🐾

Walk 20 **Alcock Tarn** - 4 miles..........................38   Grasmere   🐾🐾🐾

Walk 1 - 3 Miles
THIRLMERE

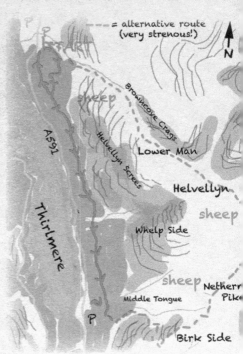

On the map:
= alternative route (very strenous!)
N
P
P
sheep
Browncove Crags
A591
Helvellyn Screes
Lower Man
Helvellyn
Thirlmere
sheep
Whelp Side
sheep
Netherr
Pike
Middle Tongue
P
Birk Side

This is an easy, low level walk, best done in Autumn when all the colours in the trees are at their best. There are no sheep on this walk, however there may be deer. You may also see Red Squirrels and a variety of birdlife!

Begin from the Swirls Car Park (Pay & Display) at NY317169. (If you don't want to pay, there is a lay-by just to the North on the right, just be very careful walking alongside the very busy A591 in order to reach the start point).

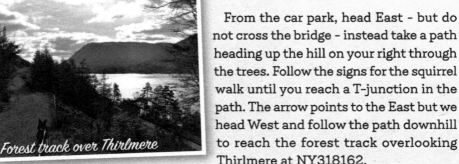

Forest track over Thirlmere

From the car park, head East - but do not cross the bridge - instead take a path heading up the hill on your right through the trees. Follow the signs for the squirrel walk until you reach a T-junction in the path. The arrow points to the East but we head West and follow the path downhill to reach the forest track overlooking Thirlmere at NY318162.

Turn left and follow the forestry track which is easy but undulating, with fine views appearing over the lake as you continue. Either walk to Homesdale Green Bridge or simply turn around before this when you have walked enough and head back the same way, staying on the forest road until you return to the car park.

On Birk Side

View to Raven Crag

Squirrel walk

Note: Super-fit dogs may wish to go up to Helvellyn, there are no stiles, but this is a **very strenuous walk** of 8 miles. There may be sheep. If you are experienced in the more strenuous walks, you can head up the steep path of Birk Side from NY327136, head North past Nethermost Pike - but ignore the large path to the summit of Helvellyn, follow the edge of the cliff instead to get the best views of Striding Edge. Once you have visited Helvellyn summit, head NW to Lower Man and Browncove Crags, returning back to the car park via a very steep descent on a rocky path to Helvellyn Gill.

View to High Seat

Striding Edge

Walk 2 - 5 Miles
SHIVERY KNOTT

This quiet walk takes you through woodland to the boggy but worthwhile 'summit' of Shivery Knott. If you wished to do a longer walk however, you could also summit Ullscarf from here, or descend to Blea Tarn for a picnic!

Begin from the pay & display car park at Dobgill Bridge, with your dog on a lead as there may be sheep ahead. There is a path leading directly from the car park up the hill into the trees, but we walked up the road to the North to NY316142, where a path leads through interesting moorland up the steep slope to a forest track and a deer gate at NY313144.

Deer Gate

Pass through the deer gate and head South-West along the track. It's safe to let your dog off now though despite the deer gates, you may encounter deer! Follow the track and take a left turn at a fork to visit Harrop Tarn.

When you are ready, return to the path and head West uphill to another deer gate at NY303138. Putting your dog on a lead now, head through the gate into the moorland. You may see deer and sheep here.

Tarn on Shivery Knott

Deer

Near Harrop Tarn

Shivery Knott

Follow the boggy path up the hill to the West. Where the ground levels, you have a choice of paths, we went to the North and enjoyed the view from an un-named summit near Shivery Knott, but if you choose you may wish to head South to Ullscarf which will add an extra couple of miles to your journey, or even drop down to Blea Tarn which is a quiet, delightful tarn where you may occasionally see fish leaping! It's a nice spot for lunch before returning to the car by the same way you came up.

Note: Do not attempt to take what appears to be a bridleway down to Binka Stone from Harrop Tarn as this is a very steep, bouldery and slippery path through spiky shrubs containing sheep. It must have been some horse that traversed that way in times gone by!!

Fun in the forest stream

Walk 3 - 9 Miles
POOLEY BRIDGE

This walk begins with a lovely steamer trip across the beautiful Lake Ullswater. A favourite with many people, you will need an early start to avoid the crowds. In Pooley Bridge, park just North of the landing stage in a Pay & Display car park by the river before the bridge. Catch the ferry (which involves no tricky steps!) and disembark at Howtown.

Head to the road then carefully walk South towards Howtown. You are looking for a path on the left beside a stream at NY443197.

Follow this path, which is delightful in Spring when the daffodils are out, past the houses to a track, which has a signpost with a person, horse and bicycle on it.

Fun on the Ullswater Steamer

Howtown

Helvellyn Range

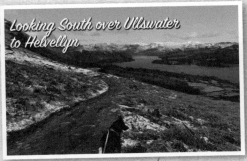
Looking South over Ullswater to Helvellyn

Daffodils by Pooley Bridge

Bridleway below Arthurs Pike

View to Fusedale

Head North East now along the bridleway, keeping your dog on a lead as sheep are kept on the moor from now until the end of the walk.

The bridleway rises steadily now with superb views of the lake and the Martindale fells behind you. Simply stay on this track until you pass Barton Park wood on your left. You cross a stream at NY473221, which is a lovely spot to have lunch.

The path continues to rise but as you reach a junction of paths at 'The Cockpit' marked on the OS 1:25000 map, turn left and head across the moor to the North, to join another bridleway, marked 'Pooley Bridge 1¼ miles' on a signpost, where you turn left and head down the hillside to join

Path to Pooley Bridge from The Cockpit

a minor road. Follow the minor road and go straight on at the crossroads. Turn left when you reach the church on the main road and stop off to buy souvenirs or perhaps have a meal in the local pub before crossing the bridge back to the car park.

Walk 4 - 4 Miles
GOWBARROW PARK

This is a very popular walk with visitors and has sheep throughout. However, it is worth mentioning as it is a great little walk with fabulous views for relatively little effort!

Begin the walk at the National Trust Pay & Display car park in the old quarry (which used to be free!) halfway up the A5091 at NY397211. Cross the road and with your dog on a lead, go through a gate and follow a gravel path to the East which takes you down to the river. Cross the river via the bridge and follow a pleasant path through the trees to the North along the Ullswater Way.

Look for a signpost just before a wall marked 'Airy Crag Gowbarrow Summit', and turn right here. Climb up the hill, which can be very boggy, and follow the path by Airy Crag, which turns South to lead you to the summit of Gowbarrow Park, which has some lovely views.

When you are ready to move on, head East down a well made path which brings you out near the woods at Kirsty Brow. Turn right again and follow the path along the edge to the South, being careful as there are some steep drops.

Turn off for Gowbarrow Fell

View to Kirksty Brow

Gowbarrow Fell summit

The path pleasantly winds its way to a memorial seat and a fence. It is worth going through the gate in the fence to admire the views and perhaps have lunch. From here, head to the West along the path which heads gently downhill. Follow the signs for Aira Force, which is one of the most stunning of the Lakeland waterfalls.

It can get very busy here, especially in summer. You may be lucky and spot some Red Squirrels in the trees. After viewing the falls, take the steep steps to the right of the waterfall and climb to the bridge.

From here it doesn't matter whether you cross the bridge or not, as we are heading North now until we reach the wooden bridge we crossed at the beginning of the walk. Retrace your steps over the field and back to the car park.

Aira Force

Looking North over Ullswater

Standing on Yew Crag

Walk 5 - 6 Miles
GRISEDALE VALLEY

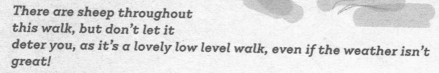

Helvellyn
Hole-in-the-wall
Nethermost Cove
Eagle Crag
Sheep
Glenridd
Sheep
← Grisedale Tarn
Sheep
St Sunday Crag
Birks
Sheep
STA
A592

N

There are sheep throughout this walk, but don't let it deter you, as it's a lovely low level walk, even if the weather isn't great!

B egin from the car park opposite the Patterdale Hotel (where the bus turns round). It's a pay & display car park which only accepted coins at the time of writing (£4.50 for the day).

Cross the road with care and go round the back of the Patterdale Hotel by walking to the right of the building. Head SW away from the back of the building and pick up a footpath through trees which leads to a gate. Keeping your dog on a lead, go through the gate and turn right. Follow an undulating path to NY387157, where you will see a path junction.

Ullswater

A wide track leads to a gate on your right, whilst another path heads steeply uphill. (The path on the left heads up to Thornhow End and St Sunday Crag). Take the track downhill to the gate and pass through, being careful as there may be traffic on the single track road.

Once on the road, turn left and head SW to a sharp right turn. Turn right here and cross the bridge over Grisedale Beck. Continue North along the road a short distance, where you will see a gate ahead going into a field.

Place Fell from below Oxford Crag

View to Hole in the Wall path

Below Thornhow End

Elmhow Plantation

Go North through the gate and up a short, steep, grassy section to another gate by a wall. Go through the gate and turn left.

Continue West along the footpath, ignoring another track which leads off up the hill to your right. Stay on the lowest footpath which winds its way past Broomhill Plantation up the valley, until you cross a footbridge at Nethermostcove Beck (NY361144).

If you want to add another couple of miles onto your walk, you can continue up the hill to Grisedale Tarn and have lunch there, before returning to this path junction.

Otherwise, look for a path on your left which goes down to the river and go across the bridge. The path is boggy and indistinct here. Carefully head NE until you join a large bridleway. Follow the bridleway to the NE back down the valley until you rejoin the minor road at Thornhow. You may encounter cows along this section.

Follow the minor road – this time do not turn off it but continue down the hill until you reach a sharp left hand bend by some cottages (Home Farm). On your right you will see yellow footpath signs – follow these through the boggy fields to the East, where you will pass through another gate and rejoin the path you started out on. Turn left after the gate and then left again through another gate to bring you back to the hotel. If you are in need of toilets, do not go back to the hotel but continue along the path which will bring you out by the public toilets next to the Post Office and the pub car park.

Eagle Crag

Nethermost Cove Beck

Broomhill Plantation

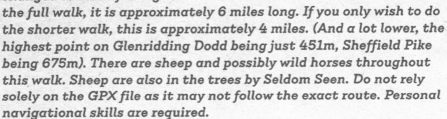

Glencoyne

Seldom Seen

Sheffield Pike

Glenridding Dodd

A592

Glenridding Screes

= alternative route

Glenridding

START

N

Walk 6 - 6 Miles
SHEFFIELD PIKE

This walk may be changed to suit. If doing the full walk, it is approximately 6 miles long. If you only wish to do the shorter walk, this is approximately 4 miles. (And a lot lower, the highest point on Glenridding Dodd being just 451m, Sheffield Pike being 675m). There are sheep and possibly wild horses throughout this walk. Sheep are also in the trees by Seldom Seen. Do not rely solely on the GPX file as it may not follow the exact route. Personal navigational skills are required.

Begin from the National Trust Pay & Display car park at Glencoyne Bridge. Head South on the permissive path beside the fields until you can go no further. Cross the road carefully then continue South on a thin, undulating path overlooking the lake (some steep drops here). After approximately 100 yds at the brow of the hill, cross the

Glencoyne

road again and follow a signposted track beside a bus stop leading West through the trees. Ignore a track leading off to the right and follow the main path over a cattle grid with a gate beside it. You often see Red Squirrels here, sheep and possibly deer.

Dawn over Ullswater

Follow the track round to the right and keep the cottages at Seldom Seen on your right. Continue West up the hill to a wall at the end of the tree line. Pass through the gate and turn left. Take the path leading up the hill beside the wall and small stream to the South (there may be horses here), which is steep in places. Be careful of the grass, which may be slippy where the water has run off the mountain. Once at the brow of the hill stop for a breather and have a good look around, the views are fabulous!

Marker post

Continue to follow the faint path beside the wall which levels out and passes a hole in the wall. Note on your right here a very faint path leading off to the right which is one of the ways up onto Sheffield Pike.

On Sheffield Pike

To visit Glenridding Dodd, continue to head South beside the wall until you drop downhill to another break in the wall. On your right here is the second path to the summit of Sheffield Pike. There are some great views over the lake and towards Kirkstone Pass from here. In front of you, you will notice the summit knoll of Glenridding Dodd beside the corner of the wall, which is reached by a well-worn rocky path (The path is very boggy in parts, but a lot easier than it looks!). As you reach the corner in the wall note the well-trodden path which heads downhill to the South and to the right another very thin path which is a third route to the summit of Sheffield Pike (not recommended). The path to the South takes you down to Glenridding village but though there are

Boggy Path view to Catstye Cam and Raise

CONT'D ON NEXT PAGE

no stiles it's not recommended as it is very steep and rocky, especially near the bottom.

Once you get onto the summit of Glenridding Dodd it's worth walking beyond it along the grassy boggy path, which brings you to the very edge and some amazing views. Be very careful though as the drop is very steep and goes down a long way!

View to Catstye Cam and Striding Edge

If you only wish to do this walk, you may either a) return the same way or b) head down the very steep rocky path into Glenridding. (There's an intermittent lakeside path to the North of the village (the Ullswater Way) which is very pleasant and takes you back to the start point).

If you wish to continue onto Sheffield Pike, visit the summit of Glenridding Dodd and then look for a path leading to the West up past Heron Pike and on to the summit. It is very steep in places. Though it would mean retracing your steps, I would probably recommend the first of the three paths mentioned.

The summit of Sheffield Pike is often overlooked, being so close to its more famous neighbours of Catstye Cam and Helvellyn. But the views here are spectacular!

When you are ready, continue NW down a very peat-boggy path to the col at Nick Head. On the way you may notice a signpost marked 'M 1912'.

This marks an old boundary agreed by the landowners of the time. At the crossroads in the path, turn right and go down the narrow but well-laid path along Bleabank Side, which will eventually take you back to the point where you turned off at the tree line. Follow the path back through Seldom Seen and to the car park (if you cross the road at the car park there is a small bay where your furry friends can go and play in the lake).

Ullswater from Seldom Seen

Walk 7 - 7 Miles
ANGLE TARN

This walk begins from a small car park at Hartsop village (NY409131) which is free but there is a donations box which you may wish to contribute to. There are sheep and deer throughout this walk.

From the car park head East along the bridleway. Cross the river and continue East up the track which traverses the hillside beneath Gray Crag, until you meet another footbridge just before Hayeswater.

Cross the bridge and head up the steep grassy slope towards The Knott, marked as a bridleway on the OS 1:25000 map. At the T junction, turn left and follow the path NW, which is boggy in places. I have often seen red deer here. Your dog may be tempted to leap into pools along the way, but it is not advised as they may find themselves up to the hilt in smelly peat bog!!

Continue past Satura Crag and down to Angle Tarn, which is a lovely spot to have lunch and hang around awhile. If you are into wild camping, the Western side of the tarn has a few dry spots on which to pitch your tent.

Angle Tarn

When you are ready, continue North along the well-worn path past Angletarn Pikes, Stony Rigg and Rake Crag down to Boredale Hause. After admiring the views over Ullswater, follow a bridleway leading down to the South then at the bottom of the fell, turn left again and continue South along the bridleway until you reach the village of Hartsop. Turn left once more and follow the minor road back to the car park.

On Satura Crag

Walk 8 - 5 Miles
PLACE FELL

This is a short but demanding walk with incredible views. It often stays dry and cloud free as the Helvellyn range tends to hug the bulk of the cloud, which mostly approaches from the West. As with much of the Lake District, there are sheep throughout this walk.

Begin from the car park opposite the Patterdale Hotel, where the bus turns round (NY397159). This was a pay & display car park which only accepted coins at the time of writing (£4.50 for the day).

With your dog on a lead, head South along the road, being careful as the road narrows on a blind bend past the White Lion pub. Past the pub a short distance on the left is a bridge and minor road heading NE to the hamlet of Rooking.

Cross the bridge and head up the road, following it round to the left. After going uphill for a short distance, take a gate on the right which leads onto the moorland. Head uphill on a path to the right which climbs steadily. The path forks, but it doesn't matter which you take as both paths converge later on.

Follow the path steadily uphill to the South until you reach Boredale Hause. Take a well-deserved rest here as we now turn left and find a path which climbs steeply to the summit of Round How.

Patterdale

The White Lion Inn

North from Place Fell

The path flattens out here and it is a pleasant walk over to the rocky summit cairn of Place Fell. The views are amazing!

Return via the same route, or, if you are fit enough, you may wish to continue heading North along the track to a sheepfold at NY414179, where we turn left and head down the hill until it joins a bridleway (The Ullswater Way) at the lakeside. Turn left here and follow the bridleway beside the lake until you reach Side Farm, who sell refreshments from a small shop. In the farmyard turn right and follow the road across the fields to pop out onto the A592 at the schoolhouse. Turn left and the car park appears on the left after a few hundred yards. (This alternative route is almost 8 miles long).

Brotherswater from Place Fell

Glenridding from Boredale Hause

View to Glenridding

Glenridding and Helvellyn Range from Place Fell

Misty's Mini Guides

Walk 9 - 4 Miles
SILVER POINT

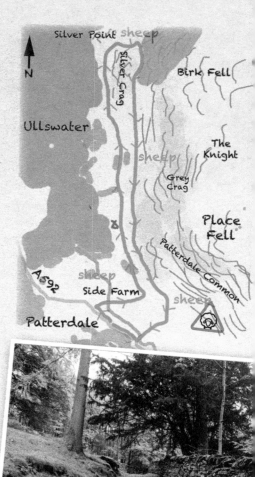

A very easy walk which can be extended to Howtown by having a trip on the Ullswater Steamer. (See note below). There are sheep scattered on the fell throughout this walk.

Begin from the car park on the opposite side of the road to the Patterdale Hotel (NY397159). It is a pay & display and at the time of writing the machine only takes coins.

Carefully head North along the A592 until you reach the school on your right. Turn right here and follow the wide track to Side Farm.

On arrival at the farm, go past the farm buildings and turn left at

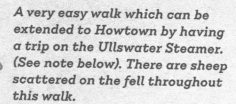
Path by Side Farm

a T-junction. Pass through the gate and continue North, following the undulating bridleway to Silver Bay. Spend awhile here then either head back the same way or look for a path rising steeply to the left of Silver Crag. Follow this then head South along the path until you reach a disused quarry (NY401162).

Lakeside path near Silver Bay

Continue South for a short distance and take a gate on your right which leads onto a minor road at Rooking. Follow this Southwards down a hill and follow the bend of the road to the right, which will bring

View to Glenridding

Path to Side Farm

Glenridding & Sheffield Pike

you across a bridge and back to the main road in the village of Patterdale. Turn right here past the pub (careful as the road narrows and the road is busy). The car park appears on the right.

Note: If extending the walk to Howtown, from Silver Point continue North along the Ullswater Way footpath until you reach the pier at Howtown. If travelling by boat first, park at the Glenridding Steamer pier (pay & display) and travel on the boat to Howtown. Head South along the Ullswater Way footpath. This will make the walk approx 6.5 miles long. It's a popular one with visitors! If you enjoy a glass of wine we recommend visiting the Glenridding mini market, which is by the post box and beside the excellent Catstycam shop, they hopefully still sell Lindesfarne wines which are delicious! (Especially the cherry one!!!).

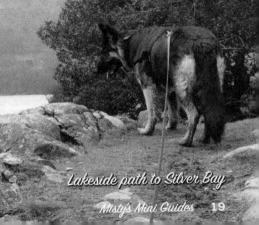

Fun in Silver Bay

Lakeside path to Silver Bay

Walk 10 - 5 Miles
SWINESIDE KNOTT

The map shows locations including Dockray, Dowthwaitehead, Bracken How, STAR, Common Fell, Watermillock Common, Swineside Knott, Spying How, Bell Knott, Aira Landing, Ullswater, with roads A5091 and A592. Labels read "untested path" and "= alternative route (untested)".

This is a quiet and pleasant walk which will get you away from the crowds and has fabulous views too! It will likely have sheep throughout the walk however and also a bit of road walking.

Park at the National Trust Pay & Display car park halfway up the A5091 at NY397211. Do not take the path rising to the SW from the car park beside a wall as there is a stile half way up! Instead, walk carefully to the North up the hill along the road until you reach the hamlet of Dockray.

Look for a path on your left beside a house at NY393215. Follow this to the SW onto open moorland. The path begins as a farmer's track but after about 100yds a faint grassy footpath bears off to the SW, which we follow to a wall at NY387205. Follow the thin path beside the wall to the SW beneath Common Fell, Swineside Knott and Brown Hills.

There is a path heading steeply downhill past Spying How which you may fancy following back to the road if you wished to visit Aira Force. A walk North along the river after viewing this will lead you back to a path which takes you to the car park (see the Gowbarrow Fell walk on page 9).

View South from below Swineside Knott

Raise & Bleabank Side from Brown Hills

Looking over Ullswater to Place Fell

I have not yet tested the path beneath Spying How for stiles or other obstacles, however.

Alternatively, continue on pathless, possibly boggy terrain to the NE back over the summit of Swineside Knott onto Watermillock Common and Common Fell, before rejoining the path you came up on and head back to Dockray, then it's a walk on the road back to the car park.

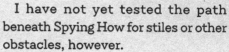
View to Raise and Bleabank Side from Brown Hills

View North from below Swineside Knott

Walk 11 - 4 Miles
STONY COVE PIKE

This walk begins with a bit of a steep scramble which your dog may/may not be able to manage. There will be sheep throughout this walk. Best done on a clear day to get the most out of the day!

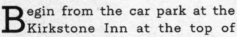

Begin from the car park at the Kirkstone Inn at the top of Kirkstone Pass on the A592. Head to the left of the Inn across the moor and go through a gate leading up the fell past some small windmills. It's a stiff climb of 200m with a bit of scrambling near the top. Once you are past this part it's a pleasant walk across peat bog and grassy tracks to the North along St Raven's Edge.

You will head downhill slightly then up again onto Pike How and John Bell's Banner. There's some amazing views to the South, it's worth pausing as you go to have a look around!

Up on Caudale Moor you will find some lovely spots for lunch, with fantastic views to the North over Ullswater and Place Fell. You can walk as far as you like, perhaps continue to Thornthwaite Crag and High Street if you are feeling energetic.

For this walk however, we go as far as Stony Cove Pike and enjoy the views before heading back the way we came.

St Ravens Edge

Tricky section

Boggy bit

View to Brotherswater from Caudale Moor

Walk 12 - 3 Miles
RYDAL WATER

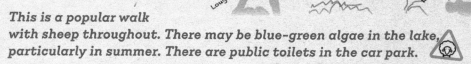

This is a popular walk with sheep throughout. There may be blue-green algae in the lake, particularly in summer. There are public toilets in the car park.

Begin from the Pay as you Leave car park at NY351065. Carefully cross the busy A591 and head North on a bridleway to NY347068. Turn right onto another bridleway signed 'Coffin Route to Rydal' and follow this to the East.

There are some lovely views all along here but remember there are sheep in most of the fields. After about a mile you come to the lovely village of Rydal. There are some lovely places to explore here which you may like to divert to, such as Rydal Hall which is dog-friendly and has great waterfalls in the gardens.

Go to the A591 once more and turn right. Carefully cross the road, looking for a path on the left which goes down to a bridge over the River Rothay. Cross the bridge then head West along an easy path beside the lake.

The path rises after Jobson Close to a junction in the path beside a ruined outbuilding. Turn right into the woods at NY349061. Head through the woods and cross the metal bridge at NY348064. Head to the East and return to the car park.

Walk 13 - 7 Miles*
EASEDALE TARN

🐾 🐾 🐾 🐾

This walk begins from any of the pay & display car parks in Grasmere (or your accommodation should you be staying there!). There are sheep throughout this walk.

Head North through the village to a junction marked by a telephone symbol on the OS 1:25000 map at NY337076. Head NW through Allan Bank park then North where the path forks to take you to Easedale Road. Follow Easedale Road NW until you reach a right-hand bend with a slate bridge across Easedale Beck.

Cross the bridge and continue NW along a very wide cobbled bridleway, which is popular with visitors. Continue NW, taking in the views towards Sourmilk Gill Waterfalls. The path leads steeply up the hill and past the falls, then turns West, bringing you out suddenly at Easedale Tarn.*

Most of the visitors stop here, and the area around the tarn begins to get very boggy. Follow the path Westwards and climb carefully up to Belles Knott. At Belles Knott cross the stream via stepping stones then head North to visit the lovely and unfrequented Codale Tarn. A great place for lunch!

At Codale Tarn

View to Helm Crag

Far Easedale

Path from Stythwaite Steps

The thin path disappears now as we head North from Codale Tarn and make our way to Tarn Crag, where a path reappears and leads East to the summit of Tarn Crag at NY304093. The views from here are superb and you are unlikely to encounter many other people.

Easedale Tarn

Continue East along the path to Greathead Crag, and continue down the hill between Stenners Crag and Cockly Crag. The path becomes more distinct now as we head North beneath Stenners Crag to Stythwaite Steps at NY318094.

Sourmilk Gill waterfall

Cross the wooden footbridge and head SE along the rocky bridleway, which eventually brings you out at a junction with the path to Helm Crag on your left.

Turn right at Lancrigg and then left onto Easedale road, which is followed back to Grasmere.

Slate Bridge

If you wish to do a much shorter walk, cross the river at Easedale Tarn and head East along a well-defined footpath beneath Cockly Crag and Stenners Crag to bring you out at Stythwaite Steps. Follow the route thereafter as described in the last two paragraphs.

Walk 14 - 6 Miles
SILVER HOW

This is one of my favourite walks, and surprisingly overlooked by the crowds, though it is one of the worst for sheep, especially in summer! There are sheep throughout the whole of this walk and navigational skills are essential.

Parking is available in several Pay & Display car parks in Grasmere. Beginning from the church in at NY337074, head West along the minor road past a hotel, for about 450m, until you see on your left a café which is on the lakeshore with boats on a small landing stage at NY334072.

Boats at cafe landing stage

Turn right and head up a path through a gate which continues between walls to another gate, which leads out onto the moorland and then another gate where we turn left and go up the hill on a wide, rocky path beside a wall. Lovely views over Grasmere and Rydal Water emerge as you climb. At NY327064 turn right and climb the steep path which brings you to the summit of Silver How.

Lakeside Road to West of Grasmere

That's the hardest part over with now, so rest and soak in the lovely views before striking off NW along a boggy path to the West of Brigstone Moss and Lang How. It is worth making detours at the largest tarns to peek over the Western edge of the fell, as there are some beautiful views here overlooking the Langdale Valley and the Langdale Pikes.

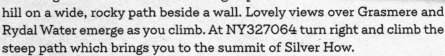

Continue along the summit to the West of Swinescar Pike. If you feel you have walked far enough, look for a path on the right here (at NY312071) and descend via Swinescar Hause and Blindtarn Gill to join the busy Easedale path at NY326083. (This walk is about 5 miles long).

Grasmere & Rydal Water from Silver How

The path to Blea Rigg from Silver How

Misty looks over the Langdale Valley

If you're still keen to go on, continue past Little Castle How until you reach the tarns at Great Castle How.

Do not ascend Blea Rigg, but turn right at NY303077 and follow a path down through bracken to Easedale Tarn.

Be careful as it becomes very boggy as you approach the tarn. I once nearly lost a walking stick trying to keep my balance there!!

Turn right onto the well-worn path by the tarn and head East, following the busy path which runs beside Sourmilk Gill.

Continue down the path to the East, it is fairly steep in places but nothing too difficult! Upon reaching the valley continue SE via Easedale until you reach Easedale Road, which is followed back into Grasmere.

Walk 15 - 3 Miles
LOUGHRIGG FELL

A short walk but with a very steep section! There are several ways this hill can be tackled so you may wish to choose alternative ways. There are sheep throughout this walk. There may be blue-green algae in the lake, particularly in summer.

We began from the Pay as You Leave car park at NY351065. There are public toilets here. Head West along a lovely footpath to the river and a pretty footbridge. Cross the footbridge and head up the hill to the South through the trees. Upon reaching a gate, pass through this and turn right onto a path beside the wall until you reach a fork in the path.

Take the left hand path onto Loughrigg Terrace, then as you walk, look for another path on the left which dog-legs back up the fell. This is very steep in places but eases off at NY346055 and becomes a pleasant path through interesting scenery, until the summit is reached.

Grasmere

In the woods approaching Loughrigg Terrace

There are some amazing views from here, and it is fun to explore the lumpy summit! You may wish to descend by a different route, but for ease of explanation I chose to return to the Loughrigg Terrace path by the same route I climbed.

Instead of following the Terrace however, continue straight on into the woodland at Red Bank. (High Close Estate, Deerbolts Woods, owned by the National Trust). Follow the path down to the lakeside then head East to a footbridge over the river.

Pretty footbridge

You may choose which side of the river to return on, the path on the other side of the bridge is very wide and easy to follow, but the one on the South side of the river is thinner, undulating, with several twists and turns and places to explore.

Heading for Ewe Crag from Loughrigg

Both paths return you to the pretty footbridge at the beginning of the walk. Simply retrace your steps to the East and return to the car park.

Path back to the car park

View North from Loughrigg

Walk 16 - 5 Miles
BROTHERS WATER

This is a stunning low-level walk suitable for all abilities. It has superb views, lakeside paths, waterfalls and lots of wildlife for the eagle-eyed There will be sheep and possibly cattle throughout this walk.

Park at the very busy but free car park at Cow Bridge (NY403134) and head South through the trees on the lakeside path, following the river which you keep on your left. There are sheep here.

Lovely views over Brothers Water appear and it is a beautiful spot to amble along. Brothers Water used to be called Broad Water, but in the 19th Century the name was changed after two brothers sadly drowned. In July there are water lilies blooming and there are often swans to be seen. The trees in the broadleaved woods house many lovely species of birds and red squirrels too. You may also see herons here.

Brotherswater

Continue along past the edge of the lake to Hartsop Hall and go through a gate. Here, the path splits. Turn left and go round the other side of the buildings then continue in an Easterly direction on a concrete road through the campsite to Sykeside Farm.

Bridleway to Dubhow

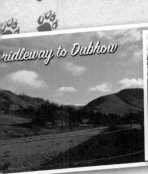
Bridleway to Dubhow

Deepdale

Dove Crag and Fairfield

Go past the buildings towards the road and look for a path to the left of the main vehicle entrance. The path runs through fields beside a wall and parallel to the busy A592. The wall is broken in places so it is best to keep your dog on a lead here.

Continue North along the path which meanders between the fields and the wall, with superb views over the valley until you reach a fence in front of you. The path goes onto the road for a few yards then drops down to the lake shore. Continue North beside the lake to a gate which appears up the hill on your right at NY405128. Immediately cross the road with care and go through a wooden gate set back from the road. Head North East down a track beside a tree-lined wall to the 17th Century village of Hartsop. Hartsop means 'valley of the deer'.

Cross the bridge over the river and turn left onto the road. Follow the road out of the village, looking for a Bridleway by a house sporting a defibrillator on your right, just before reaching the main road. Head North along the Bridleway passing wooden holiday homes and then you will pass through a gate with a lovely waterfall on the right. There will be sheep and possibly deer here. Continue North on the bridleway until you pass Dubhow.

Approximately 400m North of Dubhow you will see another Bridleway zig zagging downhill to your left and over a bridge. (NY404147). Take this and walk West to Bridgend through the fields where there are sheep. Keep your dog on a lead as you pass through another gate and beside picturesque houses, as the busy main road appears suddenly.

Carefully cross the busy A592 and head South across the bridge and past a red phone box. Ignore a footpath sign to your right and continue along the grassy verge of the road to the South for 400m.

As you approach some trees be very careful as the grass verge narrows for around 50m before the path rises near a gate and stone stile and enters woodland by means of a wooden gate. Follow the permissive and often muddy path through the trees (sheep here!) to the South which runs alongside the road back to the car park.

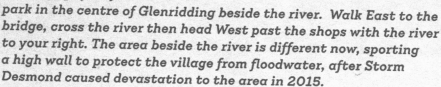

Walk 17 - 5 Miles
LANTY'S
TARN

There are sheep throughout the whole of this walk. Begin from the large pay as you arrive car park in the centre of Glenridding beside the river. Walk East to the bridge, cross the river then head West past the shops with the river to your right. The area beside the river is different now, sporting a high wall to protect the village from floodwater, after Storm Desmond caused devastation to the area in 2015.

Along this road are Catstycam and the Glenridding Mini Market. Both are excellent shops! The staff in Catstycam are very knowledgable, have an excellent range of mountain clothing and footwear and they also stock lots of things for dogs, including leads, collars and poo bags! Why not call in the mini market on your return to stock up on Lindesfarne wine and other essentials?!

Follow the road through the picturesque village and look for a path leading to your left up the hill at NY384168. It climbs steeply at first through the trees and along a stone path which zig-zags up the hill to NY384164, with fantastic views over the village.

Pass through a gate and walk beside the delightful Lanty's Tarn. Continue to the South beyond the end of the tarn to admire the fantastic views up Grisedale valley before taking a path to your right leading back up the hill to NY381162.

Go through the gate and continue straight on. The path is hard to see at first but is easily picked up again. Continue to follow the path which gradually descends to a stone footpath.

Pass by a gate on your right at NY376167 and follow the path to the West which continues up the valley, eventually leading to a footbridge at NY363173.

You may like to venture a little further up the valley here and have lunch beside the river, where there are some lovely spots and great views to Catstye Cam. (Beware of sheep!!!)

Rattlebeck Bridge

Cross the river via the bridge and head East, past the YHA buildings and down Greenside Road. In Spring there are some lovely views up Swart Beck when the gorse bushes are in flower.

Glenridding Dodd

Continue down the concrete road and look out for a signpost and gate on the right at NY373173. Head down the grassy slope to a bridge with stunning views up the valley. Cross the river and follow the sometimes muddy track to the East which eventually leads to a minor road by Rattlebeck Bridge. Turn left onto the minor road then right to pass through the campsite at Gillside. Follow the riverside path to the East which will bring you out at the village road which you started out on.

Glenridding Valley

Lantys Tarn

Walk 18 - 7 Miles

HARTSOP
ABOVE HOW

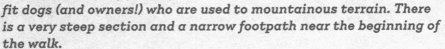

There are sheep throughout this walk. This walk is recommended only for very fit dogs (and owners!) who are used to mountainous terrain. There is a very steep section and a narrow footpath near the beginning of the walk.

Begin the walk from the free but popular car park at Cow Bridge (NY403134). Head South through a gate along a wonderful path through trees beside a river, which leads to Brothers Water. Follow the path beyond the lake to Hartsop Hall, where the path splits.

Take the path straight ahead then to the right which heads into the stunning Dovedale valley along a slightly ascending path past a disused mine and beside a wall. You may encounter cows here. The path here is rocky but pleasant and eventually leads to a very steep climb at the head of the valley to Priests Hole.

Priests Hole

Dovedale Valley

Looking back down Houndshope Cove

Looking back up Hartsop above How to Hart Crag

Hartsop above How

Brotherswater

Priest's Hole (cave) is to the South here but is not recommended with a dog as there is a very steep drop. Once you have your breath back, continue South-Westwards to the col then turn right and climb up onto Hart Crag. Turn right again here and carefully make your way down from the summit to a boggy path which leads to the

Dovedale Valley waterfalls

North-East along Hartsop above How, which is a series of boggy summits leading gradually downhill.

Pass through a gate into the woodland and continue North through the trees, through another gate then across a field to join the A592 near a phone box. Turn right here and head South carefully following a path along the verge until the path rises and enters woodland once more through a gate. Head Southwards through the trees (sheep here!) where you will return to the car park.

Fairfield from Deepdale Park

GREAT DODD

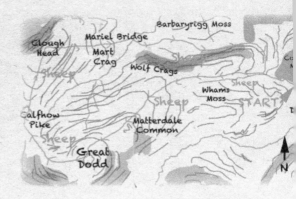

🐾 🐾 🐾 🐾

An early start is recommended for this walk as parking is free but very limited. There are sheep throughout the whole of this walk. Recommended only for dogs who are used to strenuous mountain climbs.

Park at NY381219 which is best reached via Dockray. Walk West through a gate along an obvious path beside woodland. Upon reaching a wooden footbridge, cross the river then turn immediately left and head West up the hill into open moorland.

This path can be extremely boggy around Bruts Moss and onto Randerside. Continue to the West onto the summit of Great Dodd, where there are splendid views all around. There is a wind shelter to the South of the summit where you could have lunch before taking a well-worn path to the West leading down the hill to Little Dodd.

On Great Dodd

Calfhow Pike

Mariel Bridge

Bridleway by Cockley Moor

Signpost for dogs!

Crossing Groove beck the fun way!

Near Barbary Rigg

Head North to Calfhow Pike and then up a boggy path to Clough Head, taking care here as there are some steep cliffs. Ignore the path heading Northwards, instead head East and carefully go down the hill over pathless tussocky grass to a gate at NY349227, marked Mariel Bridge on the OS 1:25000 map. There is a river here where your dog can get water.

There are some wonderful views to the North from here. Turn right and follow the Old Coach Road to the East past Barbary Rigg to a forest, where the path heads South and rejoins the large path by the bridge crossed at the beginning of the walk. Retrace your steps beside the woodland to the East to return to the car.

View North from Barbary Rigg

Walk 20 - 4 Miles
ALCOCK TARN

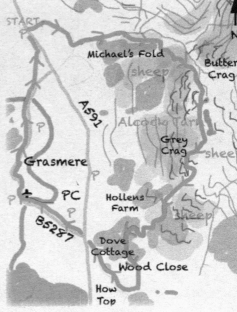

This is a delightful walk but it has some very steep climbs and descents. There may be sheep throughout. Begin the walk from the free lay-by to the North of Grasmere at NY338085. It does get full very quickly however so you may need to start from one of the town centre Pay & Display car parks and make your way to this point.

A cold Alcock Tarn

Cross the road carefully and head North-East along a minor road towards Michael's Nook. Follow the road round to the right and look for a public footpath on the left at NY341084.

Continue up the hill and stay right where the path splits. Cross the river and follow an obvious path steeply up the hill to the South, which eventually brings you to Butter Crag and some beautiful craggy landscapes which are screaming at you to explore!

View to Helm Crag from Butter Crag

Continue around the path until you come to Alcock Tarn. Spend a while here before continuing South and picking up a path to the West by Grey Crag, which descends very steeply through the moorland and eventually into trees.

Alcock Tarn

As the path levels you pop out onto a track at NY345068. Turn right to join a minor road overlooking Grasmere lake. Turn right again and follow the road past the famous Dove Cottage and carefully cross the main road at the mini-roundabout.

To Helm Crag from above Wood Close

Head into Grasmere and spend awhile exploring the many different shops and cafes if you please, before heading North after the Church to follow the B5287. Where the path forks at NY339082, go North onto the minor road then turn left at the main road and follow the kerb carefully to return to the car.

Grasmere from Alcock Tarn

Enjoying the view by Alcock Tarn

LAKELAND WALKS FOR BIG DOGS!
Series 1 - North & West Cumbria

Misty's Mini Guides

SHARON LEE

Series 2 - Central & East Cumbria

Misty's Mini Guides

...LAND WALKS
...BIG DOGS!

...RON LEEDELL

Series 3 - South Cumbria

Misty's Mini Guides

LAKELAND WALKS
FOR BIG DOGS!

SHARON LEEDELL

Misty's Mini Guides

LAKELAND WALKS FOR BIG DOGS

- 20 detailed walks in each book

- Step by step directions

- Colour photos & map of each walk

- Various distance & difficulty levels

Milton Keynes UK
Ingram Content Group UK Ltd.
UKHW020824190324
439565UK00008B/132